Grandma's Thoughts
A Guided Journal

©Beth Yarbrough

This Book Belongs To:

Once upon a time, I
was a little girl.

Yes, it was a long time ago.
No, people weren't still riding on
horses for transportation!

I can remember a great deal about
my childhood, and even
though it seems like only yesterday
to me, it may be an interesting
glimpse into the
past for someone else.

Just do me a favor and don't call it
"the olden days!"

My earliest childhood memories...

_____

_____

_____

_____

_____

_____

_____

_____

_____

_____

_____

_____

_____

_____

Important events in my life...

Important events in the world around me...

_____
_____
_____
_____
_____
_____
_____
_____
_____
_____
_____
_____
_____
_____
_____
_____

There was a day I will never forget...

The simple joys of childhood, for me, were...

There were certain people I was close to...

_____

_____

_____

_____

_____

_____

_____

_____

_____

_____

_____

_____

_____

_____

_____

_____

I felt loved when...

When I was in school, things were a little different...

YOUTHFUL HOPES
& DREAMS

Just about every girl my age,
at one point or another,
planned to grow up and move
to Hollywood and live
happily ever after.

Through the years,
the plans changed several
dozen times, but those
first hopes and dreams
were very special.

Of course, we all know
how wonderfully it turned out.

And, by the way, I am living
happily ever after!

My earliest plans for the future...

One of my most outrageous daydreams consisted of...

The first time I ever dreamed of doing what I am doing today...

I am proud of...

Some things I have always wanted to do...

THE LOVE OF MY LIFE

Sometimes, the man of your dreams really does ride into your life on a white horse.

Sometimes, he turns out to be the boy next door.

Either way, when you fall in love, it's a wild ride.

And most of the time, it's fabulous!

I remember the very first time I ever saw your grandfather...

Our first date and how it came about...

The first time I realized he was my Prince Charming...

_____

_____

_____

_____

_____

_____

_____

_____

_____

_____

_____

_____

_____

_____

Our grand scheme for conquering the world
(early hopes and dreams)

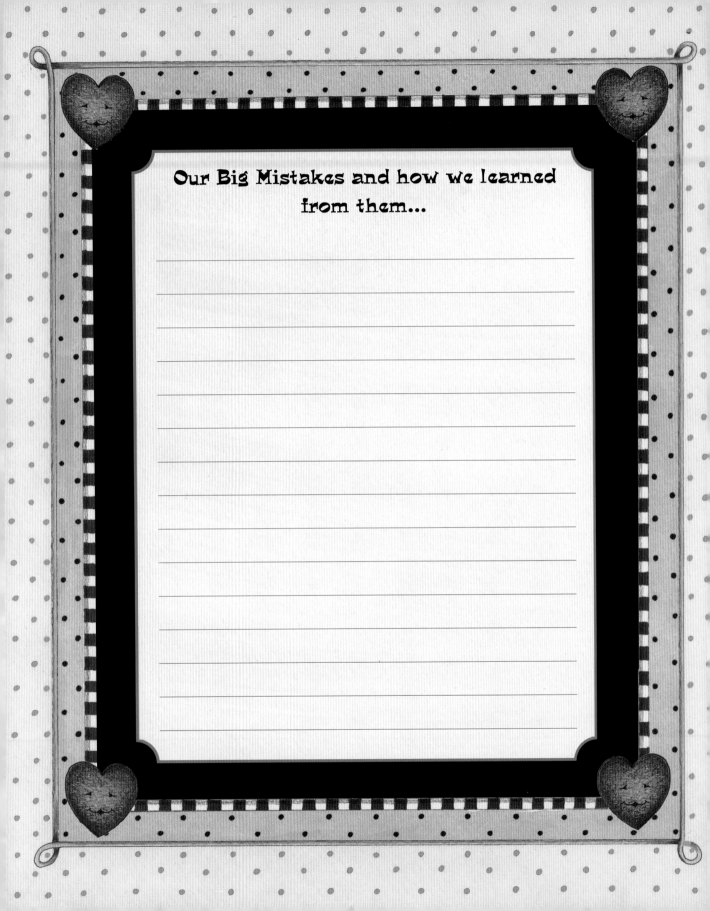

Our Big Mistakes and how we learned from them...

We make a great team because...

Our fondest desires for our children and grandchildren...

_____

_____

_____

_____

_____

_____

_____

_____

_____

_____

_____

_____

_____

_____

_____

_____

MOTHERHOOD

Busy as a Bee!

If you hold me to the truth and
ask me for my
first reaction to becoming a
mother, I will tell you it
was sheer panic.

Thankfully, it passed quickly,
and I became a pretty
spectacular Mom after all was
said and done!

Then again, don't question my
children too closely
on this point...

My first born, my first thoughts...

Sweet details that I will hold in my heart forever...

Motherhood is full of surprises.
I was most surprised by...

_____

_____

_____

_____

_____

_____

_____

_____

_____

_____

_____

_____

_____

_____

_____

Through my child, I learned about myself...

_____

_____

_____

_____

_____

_____

_____

_____

_____

_____

_____

_____

_____

_____

_____

Disasters and debacles and
how I survived...

The firsts that I will never forget...

My Mom was a great example...

Special times I spent with my children...

I laughed so hard I cried when...

If I had it all to do over again, I would...

BALANCE

No one told me life was going
to be a balancing act.

I would have paid a little
more attention when the circus
came to town.

Fortunately for me
and everyone around me, I did
learn a thing or two about
giving to others while also
nurturing myself.

Balance in my life is achieved...

_____

_____

_____

_____

_____

_____

_____

_____

_____

_____

_____

_____

_____

_____

Time just for me...

_____

_____

_____

_____

_____

_____

_____

_____

_____

_____

_____

_____

_____

Simple pleasures that bring me joy...

_____

_____

_____

_____

_____

_____

_____

_____

_____

_____

_____

_____

_____

Accomplishments that bring me satisfaction...

_____

_____

_____

_____

_____

_____

_____

_____

_____

_____

_____

_____

_____

_____

Things I have learned about who I am that were a complete surprise...

_____

_____

_____

_____

_____

_____

_____

_____

_____

_____

_____

_____

_____

_____

_____

_____

I am fortunate to have the ability to touch others through...

_____

_____

_____

_____

_____

_____

_____

_____

_____

_____

_____

_____

I would like others to describe me as...

_____

_____

_____

_____

_____

_____

_____

_____

_____

_____

_____

_____

_____

_____

I strive to...

_____

_____

_____

_____

_____

_____

_____

_____

_____

_____

_____

_____

_____

_____

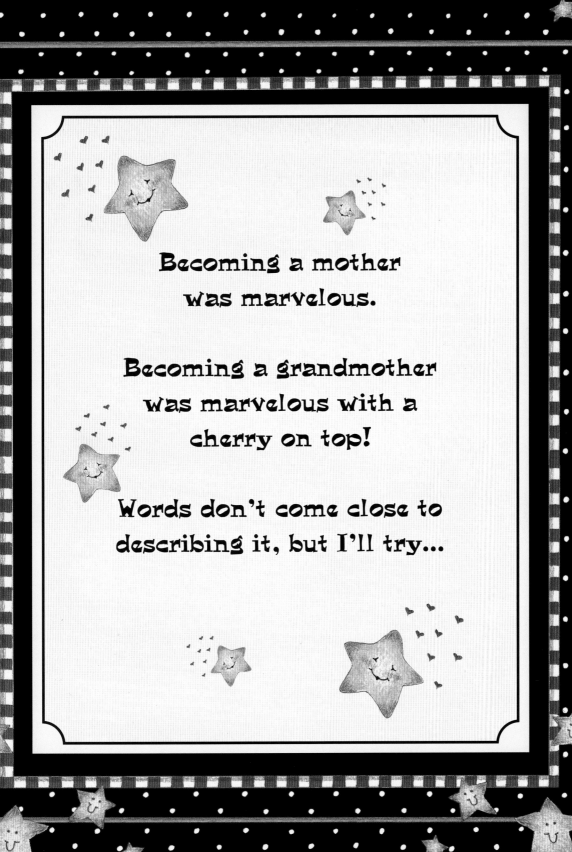

Becoming a mother
was marvelous.

Becoming a grandmother
was marvelous with a
cherry on top!

Words don't come close to
describing it, but I'll try...

When I first learned I was going to be a grandmother...

_____

_____

_____

_____

_____

_____

_____

_____

_____

_____

_____

_____

_____

_____

My totally objective account of one of the
most splendid events in modern history...
the birth of my first grandchild!

_____

_____

_____

_____

_____

_____

_____

_____

_____

_____

_____

_____

_____

_____

I went more than a little overboard...

My thoughts on watching my children become parents...

_____

_____

_____

_____

_____

_____

_____

_____

_____

_____

_____

_____

_____

The first time my grandchild said my name...

How can becoming a grandmother make me so much younger?

_____

_____

_____

_____

_____

_____

_____

_____

_____

_____

_____

_____

_____

_____

Miracles multiplied,
(or, the true story of further wondrous arrivals of more grandchildren)...

_____

_____

_____

_____

_____

_____

_____

_____

_____

_____

_____

_____

_____

_____

JOYS & WONDERS

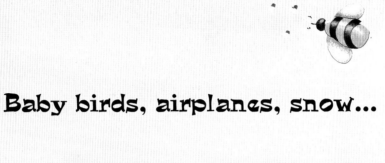

Baby birds, airplanes, snow...

simple miracles that I took
for granted until I
rediscovered them through the eyes
of my grandchildren.

It truly is a wonderful world!

Some of the first encounters with the joys and wonders of life...

_____

_____

_____

_____

_____

_____

_____

_____

_____

_____

_____

_____

I was privileged to be there when...

I see myself in my grandchildren...

Is it just me, or is this child simply extraordinary? Early signs of talent...

Important lessons they have learned...

I had forgotten how much fun it was, until...

_____

_____

_____

_____

_____

_____

_____

_____

_____

_____

_____

_____

_____

_____

_____

Technically, I am the
Grand Duchess of Kisses and Hugs, but the
grandchildren call me...

_____
_____
_____
_____
_____
_____
_____
_____
_____
_____
_____
_____
_____
_____
_____
_____

The story of how I got that name...

Memorable blabs, blurts, and mispronunciations...

If I could leave one gift with my grandchildren, it would be...

_____

_____

_____

_____

_____

_____

_____

_____

_____

_____

_____

_____

_____

_____

FAMILY TIES

Snug

as a

Bug!

©Beth Yarbrough

Building a family is a mixed bag of trauma and triumph, but the end result is well worth the effort.

Our family is no exception to the rule, and I think we are pretty spectacular, as families go.

Even before the grandchildren,
we were a team...

_____

_____

_____

_____

_____

_____

_____

_____

_____

_____

_____

_____

_____

_____

How my children's spouses have enriched our lives...

When they needed me, I was there. Memorable
times I was able to give support to my family.

And they needed me when...

_____

_____

_____

_____

_____

_____

_____

_____

_____

_____

_____

_____

_____

_____

I remember these special times when our whole family got together...

_____

_____

_____

_____

_____

_____

_____

_____

_____

_____

_____

_____

_____

How the grandchildren have made our circle complete...

_____

_____

_____

_____

_____

_____

_____

_____

_____

_____

_____

_____

_____

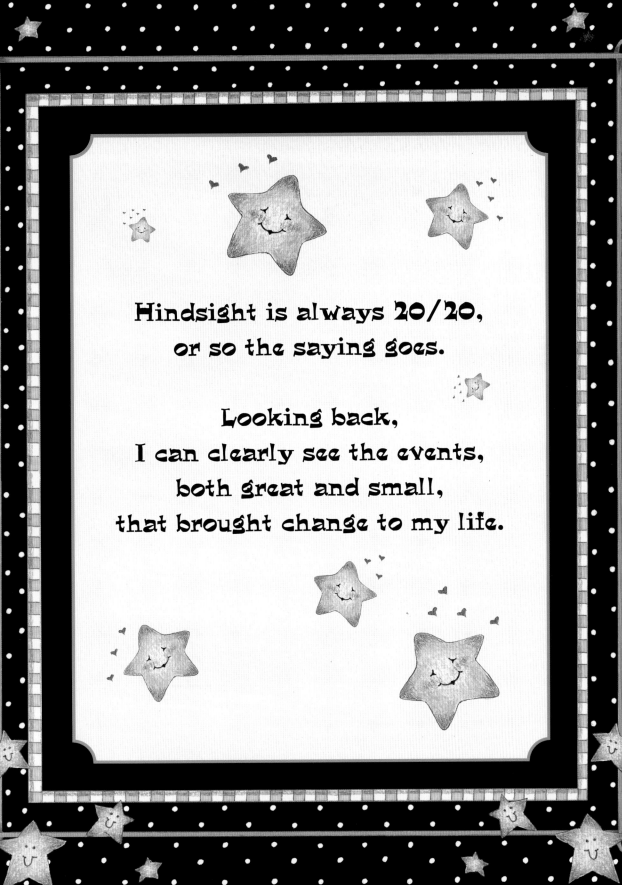

Hindsight is always 20/20,
or so the saying goes.

Looking back,
I can clearly see the events,
both great and small,
that brought change to my life.

There was a fork in the road, and I chose...

Small coincidences that had major effects...

_____

_____

_____

_____

_____

_____

_____

_____

_____

_____

_____

_____

_____

_____

Travels, and how they have enriched and changed me...

_____

_____

_____

_____

_____

_____

_____

_____

_____

_____

_____

_____

_____

_____

Times when I did the the right thing at great cost...

_____

_____

_____

_____

_____

_____

_____

_____

_____

_____

_____

_____

People who have influenced and inspired me...

How I spend my free time...

_____

_____

_____

_____

_____

_____

_____

_____

_____

_____

_____

_____

_____

THE FUTURE IS BRIGHT

When driving down the road, it's
better to focus out
the windshield than into the
rearview mirror.

Confucius didn't say that, but if
there had been cars in his day,
he probably would have.

In any case, it's the truth.
Learn from the past, but
embrace the future!

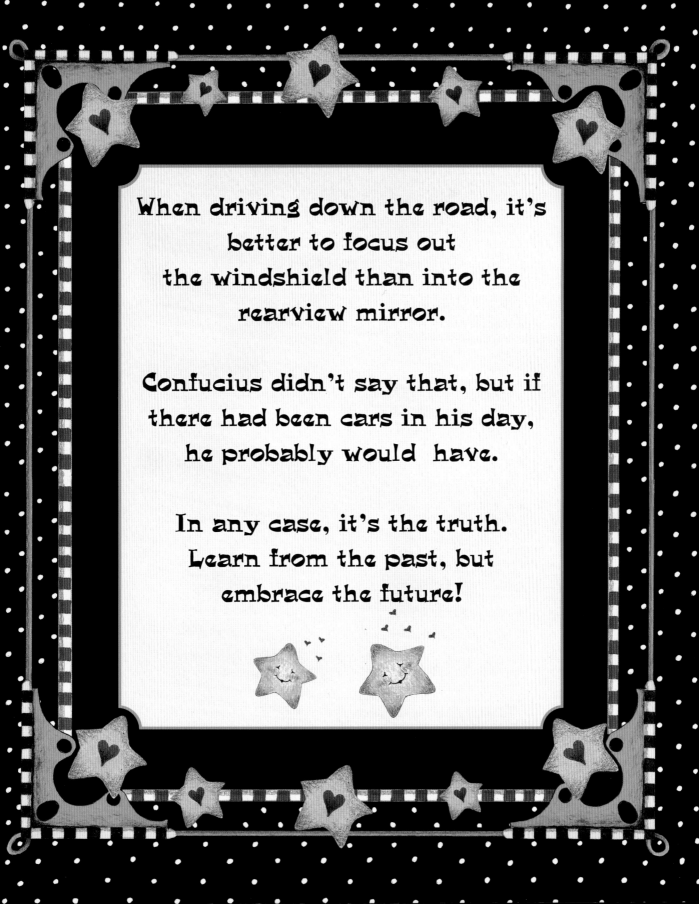

How I can make the world
a better place...

_____

_____

_____

_____

_____

_____

_____

_____

_____

_____

_____

How I can make myself a better person...

_____

_____

_____

_____

_____

_____

_____

_____

_____

_____

_____

_____

_____

_____

Things about myself I have learned to accept and enjoy...

_____

_____

_____

_____

_____

_____

_____

_____

_____

_____

_____

_____

Each day holds surprises. How I have
learned to adjust and adapt...

My goals for the future...

I am blessed because...